D1256277

Martha Washington

Jennifer Strand

abdopublishing.com

Published by Abdo Zoom™, PO Box 398166, Minneapolis, Minnesota 55439. Copyright © 2018 by Abdo Consulting Group, Inc. International copyrights reserved in all countries. No part of this book may be reproduced in any form without written permission from the publisher. Abdo Zoom™ is a trademark and logo of Abdo Consulting Group, Inc.

Printed in the United States of America, North Mankato, Minnesota
052017
092017

Cover Photo: G. F. Gilman/Library of Congress
Interior Photos: G. F. Gilman/Library of Congress, 1; Everett Historical/Shutterstock Images, 4, 8–9, 9, 16; Kurz & Allison/Library of Congress, 5; Photo Courtesy of Pam Huffman, 6; J. C. Buttre/Library of Congress, 7; Library of Congress, 10, 15; North Wind Picture Archives, 11, 13, 16–17; Jean Leon Gerome Ferris/World History Archive/Alamy, 12; Shutterstock Images, 18; Dominique C. Fabronius/Library of Congress, 19

Editor: Emily Temple
Series Designer: Madeline Berger
Art Direction: Dorothy Toth

Publisher's Cataloging-in-Publication Data
Names: Strand, Jennifer, author.
Title: Martha Washington / by Jennifer Strand.
Description: Minneapolis, MN : Abdo Zoom, 2018. | Series: First ladies |
    Includes bibliographical references and index.
Identifiers: LCCN 2017931127 | ISBN 9781532120206 (lib. bdg.) |
    ISBN 9781614797319 (ebook) | 9781614797876 (Read-to-me ebook)
Subjects: LCSH: Washington, Martha, 1731-1802--Juvenile literature. |Presidents
    spouses--United States--Biography--Juvenile literature.
Classification: DDC 973.4/092 [B]--dc23
LC record available at http://lccn.loc.gov/2017931127

Table of Contents

Martha Washington was a First Lady of the United States.

Martha was the first woman to have that role. She was an example for future First Ladies.

Martha was born on June 2, 1731. She grew up on a **plantation**.

Her mother taught her to read and write. This was unusual for a girl at this time.

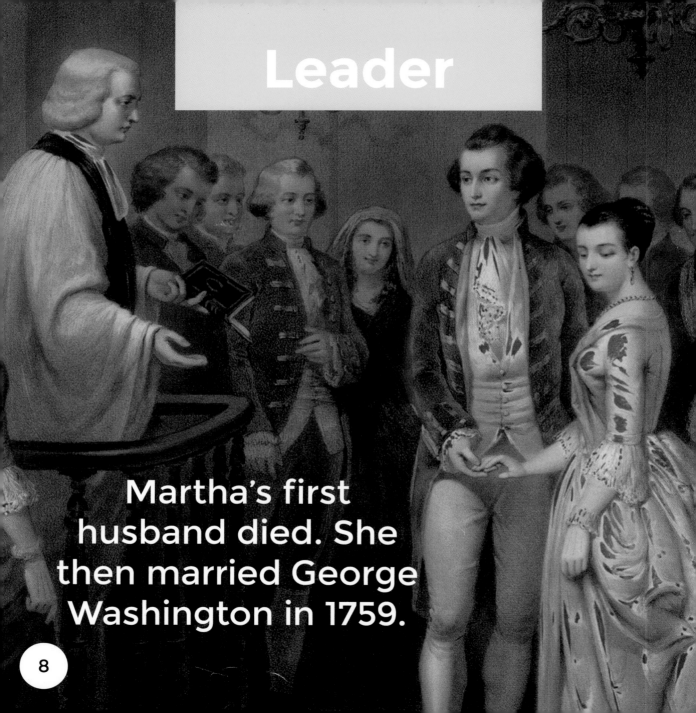

Martha's first husband died. She then married George Washington in 1759.

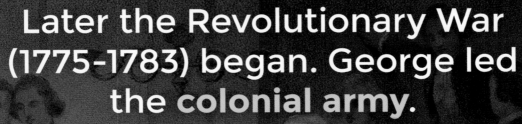

Later the Revolutionary War (1775-1783) began. George led the **colonial army.**

George was a general. Martha
lived with him at the army
camp during the winter.

She helped wives
support their husbands
who were fighting.

First Lady

In 1789 George Washington became the first US president. Martha became the First Lady.

There was no White House.
The first family lived in New York.
They later moved to Philadelphia.

Martha knew future First Ladies would follow her example. She hosted gatherings.

Both lawmakers and ordinary citizens were invited.

Martha was known for being welcoming. She made all the guests feel comfortable. Martha showed them that they were important in the new government.

17

Legacy

The Washingtons left office in 1797. They moved back to their farm in Virginia.

Martha died on May 22, 1802. She and her husband are remembered for shaping a new country.

Martha Washington

Born: June 2, 1731

Birthplace: Williamsburg, Virginia

Husbands: Daniel Parke Custis (died); George Washington

Years Served: 1789–1797

Known For: Martha Washington was the first woman to become First Lady of the United States.

Died: May 22, 1802

Key  Dates

1731: Martha Dandridge is born on June 2.

1750: Dandridge marries Daniel Parke Custis. He dies in 1757.

1759: Martha Custis marries George Washington on January 6.

1775–1783: The Revolutionary War is fought.

1789–1797: Martha Washington is First Lady. George Washington is the first US president.

1802: Martha dies on May 22.

Glossary

citizen - a person who has full rights in a country, such as the right to live there and the right to vote.

colonial army - the forces who fought for the American colonies during the Revolutionary War.

general - commander of an army.

plantation - a large farm where crops are grown to be sold.

lawmaker - a person who makes laws.

Booklinks

For more information on **Martha Washington**, please visit abdobooklinks.com

Zoom In on Biographies!

Learn even more with the Abdo Zoom Biographies database. Check out **abdozoom.com** for more information.

Index